"These powerful testimonials demonstrate faith and resilience in the face of life's challenges. I'm inspired by these stories and by all the members of our field who strive to live in service of others and who seek opportunities to lift up others along the way."

Tim Gerend, chairman, president, and CEO, Northwestern Mutual

TURNING POINTS

TURNING POINTS

FOREWORD BY
DWAAN BLACK

INTRODUCTION BY
MARK KULL

Christian Fellowship Community®

Copyright © 2025 by Christian Fellowship Community

While Philip Sarnecki, Gerard Hempstead, John Folkert, Paul Ludacka, Debra Blevons, and John Qualy are responsible for the substantive content, ChatGPT and OpenAI were used in converting the interviews into story form.

Turning Points

All rights reserved. No part of this publication may be reproduced, distributed or transmitted in any form or by any means, including photocopying, recording, or other electronic or mechanical methods, without the prior written permission of the publisher, except in the case of brief quotation embodied in critical reviews and certain other noncommercial uses permitted by copyright law. Neither the author nor the publisher assumes any responsibility or liability whatsoever on behalf of the consumer or reader of this material. Any perceived slight of any individual or organization is purely unintentional. The resources in this book are provided for informational purposes only and should not be used to replace the specialized training and professional judgment of a health care or mental health care professional. Neither the author nor the publisher can be held responsible for the use of the information provided within this book. Please, always consult a trained professional before making any decision regarding treatment of yourself or others.

For more information, email: brittany@christianfellowshipcommunity.org

ISBN: 979-8-218-56975-4

Many thanks to our editor, Gisèle Mix, and to our proofreader, Melisa Blok.

Scripture quotations are from the Holy Bible, New International Version®, NIV®. Copyright © 1973, 1978, 1984, 2011 by Biblica, Inc.® Used by permission of Zondervan. All rights reserved worldwide. www.zondervan.com. The "NIV" and "New International Version" are trademarks registered in the United States Patent and Trademark Office by Biblica, Inc.®

Christian Fellowship Community ("CFC") is an independent not-for-profit corporation. CFC is supported by volunteers and through donations from its participants. Neither CFC nor this event are endorsed by, affiliated with, or promoted by Northwestern Mutual.

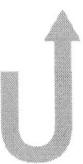

To all who have gone before us in the Christian Fellowship Community—upon whose shoulders we stand. Your faith, perseverance, and love have illuminated the path we walk today.

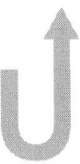

CONTENTS

Foreword by Dwaan Black 1

Introduction by Mark Kull 3

1. **Philip Sarnecki** 5
   The Journey of Truth: My Story of Faith

2. **Gerard Hempstead** 11
   My Journey of Transformation

3. **John Folkert** 15
   Overcoming Fear

4. **Paul Ludacka** 21
   A Path Guided by God

5. **Debra Blevons** 31
   Guided by Grace

6. **John Qualy** 39
   Moving God from the Trunk to the Driver's Seat

7. **Ron Joelson** 45
   Your Turning Point Opportunity

Connect with the CFC 54

History of the CFC 57

2025 CFC Board of Directors 65

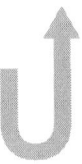

FOREWORD

What an incredible ministry and outreach the Christian Fellowship Community (CFC) is! I have become increasingly more involved with CFC over the past years, and I can honestly say it has changed my life in so many remarkable ways that it's hard to imagine not being a part of CFC. In this day and age when it is becoming more and more difficult to be your entire self in the workplace, CFC is such a breath of fresh air, allowing so many to bring who they are—including their walk of faith—to work. As believers, Jesus calls us to trust him in everything we do, to love one another, and to share the great news of the gospel with as many people as we can. My experience with CFC has shown me that mission is truly alive and well.

I believe that you will be greatly inspired as you read this collection of stories presented at the CFC Forum over the past two years. Each story is an open and reflective example of how people are choosing to bring their spirituality to their work and everything they do. We talk a lot about how idols can creep into our lives and drown out God's voice if we're not focused on our daily walk with Christ. This is a central theme in each story as the writer openly shares their experience of coming to understand how worldly idols fall incredibly short of quenching their thirst for the only relationship that can truly satisfy—a relationship with our Lord and Savior, Jesus Christ.

It takes great courage and a willingness to be different in the world to follow Jesus in every aspect of your life. Each of these stories is told with transparency, vulnerability, and sincerity. As you read them, I hope you will be inspired to reflect on your own life and faith journey.

One of the best things about CFC is the outpouring of love and the spirit of inclusion you will experience if you choose to become more involved by attending our events, such as the breakfasts at our regional and annual meetings and the monthly forums, and by engaging in a local study group taking place in many of our offices nationwide.

If you are searching to fill a void in your life, the CFC may be a great place for you. Please see the opportunities to connect at the end of this book. We would love to answer any questions you have or just be available to listen and offer understanding. Please do not hesitate to reach out. We are all on this journey together. Know that you are loved and pursued by a powerful and wonderful God, who made you perfectly in his own image.

May God bless you.
Dwaan Black

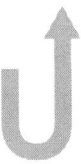

INTRODUCTION

MARK KULL

Hello reader, I am glad you are here. But more importantly, God is glad you are here. We at the Christian Fellowship Community thought it would be a great use of time and resources to share the faith journey stories of some of your peers to offer encouragement for your journey. You are going to have an opportunity to read about everyday people whose lives were changed by our extraordinary God. Some of these folks had the blessing of growing up with great parents who raised them in the church, while others had very tough lives and, through their own admissions, were complete wrecks. The beauty of the Lord is that he welcomes us all, regardless of where we see ourselves on that continuum.

Our deep hope is that you, including anyone who doesn't yet believe, will come to know God better through the ups and downs of normal individuals. By including people with various backgrounds, we hope and pray that you will connect with one of them in a way that changes your heart. As you read, you will notice that almost all our authors tried to fill a God-shaped hole in their hearts with the trappings of this world. This isn't a coincidence; it's the work of the devil. We want to help you have a *turning point*. As you will see, some turning points are dramatic and others are rather mundane. The beauty of a faith journey is that God already knows what you need; you just have to trust him.

Before you dive in, I ask you to say a quick prayer. Even if you aren't sure how to pray, God is there, and he is listening. Your prayer can be something as simple as "God, whatever your will is for my life in this moment, open my heart and mind to accept it." As you read, take time to think about when you might have been at similar points as the authors and how you responded. I hope you will see that, ultimately, the path forward to a new, different, and exciting life can be found only in a partnership with an awesome God, who loves you perfectly and unconditionally.

When you wrap up, I am guessing you will have questions or want to talk to others about that feeling we hope you experienced or the voice we hope you heard. If that's the case, just reach out. We at the Christian Fellowship Community exist to advance God's kingdom, and nothing would make us or God happier than helping you take the next step—no matter what that step is.

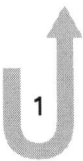

PHILIP SARNECKI

THE JOURNEY OF TRUTH
MY STORY OF FAITH

I was raised in a religious household where the early seeds of faith had been sown by my mother, who never missed a Sunday at church. Though my father wasn't initially involved, he eventually found his way back to faith. For my siblings and me, church was a nonnegotiable part of life, one that instilled in me a strong sense of morality—right and wrong, heaven and hell. But the clarity of my childhood became clouded by questions and doubts as I grew older, eventually leading me on a yearlong search that would change the course of my life.

My faith journey took an unexpected turn when I started college. I played football, and at a chapel service before my first game, Dave Angle, a speaker from Athletes in Action, delivered a message that struck a chord with me. Dave approached me afterward and invited me for a one-on-one conversation. We met at a McDonald's on campus where he asked me a life-altering question: "If you were to die today, what are the chances you would go to heaven?"

As a rule-follower and a self-proclaimed "good kid," I had always thought highly of myself. I didn't drink, smoke, or engage in reckless behavior. Confidently, I responded, "I'm about 99 percent sure." But in that moment, I realized I had been comparing myself to other people—not to the sinless standard of Jesus.

Dave pressed further: "What if that 1 percent is correct? What if you are wrong?"

These questions stuck with me. I was pragmatic by nature, so the thought of being wrong about something as important as eternity left me unsettled. Dave then explained the four spiritual laws, showing me how I could be 100 percent sure of my salvation. Although intrigued, I wasn't ready to commit just yet. Being the analytical person that I am, I needed time to process everything.

I embarked on a yearlong spiritual quest, engaging in conversations with priests, pastors, and fellow seekers and diving deep into Christian literature. Books such as *Evidence That Demands a Verdict* by Josh and Sean McDowell and *Mere Christianity* by C. S. Lewis became my companions.

Lewis's chapter on pride in *Mere Christianity* had a profound impact on me. While I had prided myself on avoiding the vices of my peers, I realized that pride itself was my greatest sin. In fact, Lewis argues that pride is the root of all sin—the sin that caused Lucifer's fall from heaven. I had been living a life of external righteousness, but internally my heart was filled with pride. It was a humbling realization. Through my reading and conversations, my understanding of faith grew. But I knew that understanding wasn't enough.

One evening during my sophomore year of college, after months of searching, I found myself alone in my dorm room. I knew I had to make a decision. It wasn't a grand or emotional moment, but it was significant. I knelt beside my bed and quietly prayed the sinner's prayer, asking Christ to come into my life and take control. From that moment on, everything changed. While life still brought its share of ups and downs, I now had a new foundation—a faith no longer based on external actions or comparisons but on the grace and forgiveness found in Jesus Christ.

As I reflect on my journey, I acknowledge that pride remained a challenge in my life, though it has lessened over time. I began to understand how pride is often a comparative sin; it's not just about having wealth or status but also about comparing ourselves to others. Even in my faith, I realized I held pride in thinking that I was better than those who engaged in certain behaviors. I came to see that this attitude was just as sinful as the actions I had been avoiding.

I also began to share with people how they could be sure of their salvation, pointing back to the four spiritual laws that had been introduced to me. Law one is that God loves us and offers a wonderful plan for our lives: "For God so loved the world that he gave his one and only Son, that whoever believes in him shall not perish but have eternal life" (John 3:16). But law two tells us that people are sinful and separated from God: "All have sinned and fall short of the glory of God" (Rom. 3:23) and "the wages of sin is death" (Rom. 6:23). Law three is that Jesus Christ is God's only provision for humankind's sin: "God demonstrates his own love for us in this: While we were still sinners, Christ died for us" (Rom. 5:8). Jesus tells us, "I am the way and the truth and the life. No one comes to the Father except through me" (John 14:6). Finally, law four is that we must individually receive Jesus Christ as our Savior and Lord: "To all who did receive him, to those who believed in his name, he gave the right to become children of God" (John 1:12).

In my conversations, I emphasized that salvation isn't something we can earn through good deeds or self-righteousness. Rather, it is a gift—a gift from God, offered through the sacrifice of Jesus Christ. "For it is by grace you have been saved, through faith—and this is not from yourselves, it is the gift of God—not by works, so that no one can boast" (Eph. 2:8–9). All that is required is for each person to receive that gift individually.

It took me a year of searching to come to this truth. But once I did, the assurance of my faith became the anchor for the rest of my life. Today, my journey of faith continues. I remain grounded in the knowledge that my salvation is not about being 99 percent sure but about being 100 percent certain—through Christ alone. And though pride may still challenge me, I face it with the same humility that led me to the truth all those years ago.

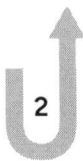

GERARD HEMPSTEAD

MY JOURNEY OF TRANSFORMATION

I was born in St. Louis and raised by loving, conservative Catholic parents who set a high standard for my siblings and me. My father, an attorney, spent his days fighting for his clients, crafting creative solutions to their legal challenges. My mother balanced her role as a homemaker with her entrepreneurial spirit, always looking for ways to contribute. Together, they instilled in my siblings and me the values of hard work, integrity, and faith.

On the surface, my childhood seemed ideal. I was an honor student, played varsity ice hockey, and even started my own lawn care business to earn extra money. My parents provided a comfortable lifestyle, and we lived in a close-knit community where we were encouraged to thrive. Yet despite this solid foundation, I found myself slipping into a life filled with sin and shame as I entered my teenage years.

When I transitioned into high school, the pressures of fitting in and the allure of the party scene began to pull me away from my upbringing. I started to lead a double life, outwardly trying to uphold my parents' values while secretly engaging in behaviors that contradicted many of the things they had taught me.

Later as a college student, I drank heavily, partied often, and became entangled in the fraternity lifestyle. My days were filled with academic responsibilities, but my nights were consumed by reckless abandon. I maintained good grades and for the most part continued attending Sunday Mass, but deep down, I was overwhelmed by guilt and confusion.

In January 1992 during winter break, my father extended an invitation that would change the course of my life. He asked me to join him on a silent retreat at a Jesuit retreat house near our home. Initially, I resisted. The idea of spending my last few days of winter break in silence with a group of "religious" men seemed dull. However, I sensed that perhaps I needed more than the distractions of my college life, so I decided to go.

That retreat became a turning point for me. The experience forced me to confront the reality of my struggles. I was surrounded by others on their own journeys of self-discovery, and for the first time, I felt a glimmer of hope amid my turmoil. As I engaged in prayer and reflection, I began to let down my guard. I realized that I was carrying the heavy weight of shame, believing the lies that the deceiver whispered in my ear: *You are unlovable. You are damaged goods. You are a lost cause.*

These thoughts had consumed me up to that point in my life, driving me into despair.

But during those moments of quiet contemplation, I began to understand something profound: God's love is unconditional. I grasped that despite my failures, I was still his beloved child, worthy of forgiveness and grace. I felt the presence of God reassuring me that I was not defined by my past mistakes. In that sacred space, I poured out my heart in confession, expressing my deep longing for redemption. I prayed fervently, asking for strength to remove the burdens of my past.

Through reconciliation, I released my sins and guilt, which allowed me to embrace the joy of forgiveness that God so freely offers.

As the retreat concluded, I knew my transformation would not happen overnight. It was a process that would take time and intentional effort. I returned to college with a renewed sense of purpose, committed to shedding the weight of my past. I began to cultivate a deeper relationship with Christ, actively seeking ways to incorporate my faith into my daily life. I attended Mass regularly, sought out Christian fellowship, and surrounded myself with positive influences who encouraged my growth.

In 1995, three years after that life-changing retreat, I married my beautiful wife, Jen. She became my partner in faith and in life, supporting me as I navigated the challenges of adulthood. Together, we built a family filled with love and support. We were blessed with three amazing children, and now two grandchildren. I can say

I am happier and healthier now than I've ever been—mentally, physically, emotionally, and spiritually.

Reflecting on my journey, I am grateful for the love and grace that have shaped my life. I have learned that transformation is not a destination but a continual process of growth and discovery. A prayer of my father's, which I recited at the retreat, still echoes in my heart: *Help us to see the many opportunities to serve you by helping others.* This call to service has become a guiding principle in my life.

Today, I strive to live out my faith, recognizing that my journey is ongoing. I share my story to inspire others who may feel lost or trapped in their own shame. I want them to know that there is always hope in Jesus Christ, who stands at the door and knocks, ready to welcome us back into his embrace (Rev. 3:20). My life is a testament to the power of forgiveness and the transformative nature of God's love.

As I reflect on my father's legacy, I see how his life was a true example of being "a man for others." His unwavering faith and dedication to helping those around him inspire me to do the same. I believe that God loves us and has an amazing plan for each of our lives, a plan filled with hope, healing, and purpose.

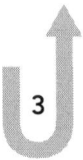

JOHN FOLKERT

OVERCOMING FEAR

I was raised in the Dutch Reformed Church, where fear was woven into nearly every sermon at any given Sunday service. I remember sitting in the pews as a kid—filled with doubt, fear, and guilt—as our pastor pounded his fist on the pulpit and pointed his finger at us, his voice booming, "What if Jesus came back today? Are you ready? Are you ready?"

I wasn't ready. I never felt ready. I'd sit there, head down, hoping I wouldn't be the one he pointed to next. Negativity, doubt, and inadequacy were what I felt during nearly every sermon. There was no talk of God's love, no community of believers encouraging one another. Instead, salvation felt like a checklist of church attendance: twice on Sundays, once on Wednesday for catechism—miss any, and your soul was in jeopardy.

I had severe ADHD as a kid, so sitting still and absorbing anything from the sermons was nearly impossible. What

I did absorb, however, was fear. I left church every week feeling small and afraid that I wasn't good enough. I grew up believing that God was angry with me, constantly waiting to catch me in my failures.

When I was older, I visited my Grampa Folkert on his deathbed. He was the epitome of what I thought a Christian man should be—kind, hardworking, devoted to his faith. But even he, lying there weak and frail, said something that haunted me: "I sure hope I've done enough to make it to heaven."

It terrified me to hear that from him. If a man like Grampa wasn't sure of his salvation, what hope did I have? The weight of guilt and shame crushed me. I wasn't just unsure—I was convinced I wasn't good enough. I carried that belief for years, like a burden I couldn't shake. It followed me into adulthood and left me feeling empty.

My fear of not being enough turned into a relentless drive to succeed. I needed to prove to myself and to the world that I had value, that I mattered. Karate became my obsession. I trained day in and day out, convinced that if I could become physically invincible, I'd finally feel powerful. I pushed myself to the edge, training six or seven days a week, year after year, chasing that black belt like it was the answer to everything.

When I finally earned it, I stood there, looking down at the belt around my waist, and waited for something to change. I expected to feel different, powerful, unstoppable. But nothing happened. I was the same person I had been the day before, just wearing a different color belt. The victory felt hollow, and the sense of inadequacy that I'd tried to crush remained.

It was the same story with my career. When I made Northwestern Mutual's Top 20 for the first time in 2008, I thought that achievement would bring fulfillment. But just as with the black belt, I reached that milestone and felt . . . nothing. No joy, no lasting satisfaction. I realized that the things of this world—success, status, accomplishments—were like "chasing after the wind" (see Ecclesiastes). No matter how much I achieved, it never filled the void inside me.

Then in the late '90s, I visited a Bible-based church that had just opened its doors in West Michigan. For the first time, I experienced something other than fear. This church wasn't about fire and brimstone; it was about love, grace, and understanding God's Word. The pastor took us through the book of Leviticus, chapter by chapter, and somehow made it incredible. For the first time, I began to feel God's love for me—not just his judgment. It was like a lifeline, pulling me out of the darkness I'd lived in for so long.

But even then, my journey wasn't without its struggles. One morning at a Bible study, a guy from our group attacked the church I had come to love. He didn't stop there; he also came after me personally. I felt my old anger flare up. I wasn't always known for my patience, and I had a temper. I held it in during the study, but when we left, I followed him into the men's room and, I'm ashamed to say, assaulted him. I was angry, defensive, and tired of feeling attacked.

A few years later, the lead pastor of this church we loved was led astray. He began focusing less on what God's divine Word states in the Bible and more on a "universalist" approach, and we could not stay. This was a huge blow to me because I thought our family had finally found what we were looking for in a church.

It was a painful wake-up call. I realized that putting my faith in people—no matter how great they seemed—was always going to end in disappointment. People are human. They make mistakes. They let you down. But God? He never fails. This pushed me to stop looking for validation from others and to focus on deepening my relationship with God.

For a while, my family and I did church at home. Every Sunday, we'd gather around and open our Bibles, and I'd lead what was likely an unimpressive family Bible study. Looking back, I'm sure my kids endured some awkward, unpolished sermons. I was no pastor, and in the middle of all this, the global war on terror was raging. I'm pretty sure many of my talks ended with "And this is why we need to eliminate Al-Qaeda," which, let's be honest, wasn't the most Christlike ending to a Bible lesson.

Eventually, we found another Bible-based church, and my faith continued to grow. Today, my relationship with God is stronger than it's ever been. I've stopped chasing achievements, stopped trying to fill that void with things that don't matter. My drive now isn't to succeed by the world's standards. My goal is to hear God say, "Well done, good and faithful servant" (Matt. 25:21, 23).

Everything I do now is about glorifying God. I'm using the opportunities and the resources I've been given to advance his kingdom, to serve others, and to grow in my faith. The things of this world—success, status, material gain—are fleeting. They never brought me joy. But walking with God? That's where I find peace, purpose, and true joy.

Looking back, I see that the fear I carried for so long was a lie from the devil. God's love, his grace—these are what are real. These are what fill the emptiness. And now, for the first time, I know that I'm walking in the right direction.

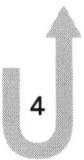

PAUL LUDACKA

A PATH GUIDED BY GOD

I didn't grow up in a home filled with love and encouragement. My first childhood memory is when I was four or five years old. My dad had been gone for several days—we didn't know where—and my mom had a dirty green laundry basket full of all his worldly possessions sitting next to the front door. When he returned, there was an altercation that escalated, and he got physical. Then my dad took that laundry basket and left, never to return. I loved my dad, but he was a drug addict and an alcoholic, and he spent most of his adult life at a local homeless shelter. He died at the age of forty-eight.

When I was eight or nine, my mom married the worst kind of abusive alcoholic I've ever known. I experienced things as a young man that most could never imagine. There were days when I'd come home from school, and I was terrified to go inside because I didn't know what was waiting for me. I'd be so scared that I'd barricade myself in my room or just hide because I was afraid of what my stepfather might do to me. And there were weeks when my mom, my brother, my four sisters, and I would have to spend three, four, or five nights a week sleeping somewhere other than our own home because it wasn't safe. Sometimes we stayed at hotels but not often because we were very poor. Other times, we bounced between friends and family. If it was nice out, we slept in the car or the back of a pickup truck and went to school the next day in the same clothes we had worn the day before.

I remember one summer day when my mom, my siblings and I, and all our neighbors stood outside our home, watching in horror as my stepfather literally destroyed our house from the inside out with a barbell. He broke every piece of glass, every piece of furniture, every wall, and every window. I wish I could tell you that was a once-in-a-lifetime event, but it wasn't. That was normal, and this was my reality.

Looking back on my childhood, the hardest part was the mental and emotional abuse. I heard words no child should ever hear—words such as "worthless" and "mistake." I was often told that I'd never amount to anything, that I was a loser, and that they wished I'd never been born. These words were often slung at me during moments of anger, but they sank into my heart and took root. For a long time, I believed them completely. Those lies became my identity.

However, when I turned fourteen, my mom and stepdad started charging me rent—$200 a month to live at home. I had to walk to my job at the local grocery store because they wouldn't drive me. I'd had to lie on my school permit and say I was a year older so I could even get the job. I started paying rent and buying my own clothes, deodorant, and toothpaste. I was pretty much self-sufficient, but I knew that my home wasn't a healthy environment. So after several months, I made a choice: I left home and moved in with my best friend and his mom (who was the closest thing to a mom I ever had).

When I first left home, I told myself, "I'm never going to drink," because I saw how alcohol destroyed not one but two families. But then I was out on my own. I saw my friends drinking, partying, chasing girls, and having a great time. I told myself, "I'm going to drink, but I'll control it," which was a lie. I began engaging in all kinds of inappropriate behavior that you wouldn't want your fourteen-, fifteen-, or sixteen-year-old doing. There were nights I drank so much that I was vomiting blood.

The one positive thing about my childhood was that I was a gifted athlete, particularly in football. It became my escape. Football was the one place where I could channel my pain into something productive. I trained hard, practiced relentlessly, and poured my heart into the game. I was always the captain of my teams, and for the first time, I felt like I was something—someone important. From the time I was eight years old until my senior year in high school, my teams collectively lost only three football games. I had big dreams: winning the state championship, getting recruited by Nebraska, winning the Heisman Trophy, and getting drafted by the Vikings. Each of these aspirations felt tangible, like my way out of the darkness.

Then, everything unraveled. It was the state championship semifinals. I had already thrown three touchdown passes and run for another. We were in double overtime, and the game was tense. On first and goal from the one yard line, I felt invincible—until, for the first time in my career, I fumbled the snap. In that split second, all my dreams shattered.

The next day, the headlines read, "Fumble Ends Indians' Great Season." I was crushed. My friends turned on me, their harsh words cutting deeper than any physical wound. "You choked! You lost the big game! You're a loser!" Their taunts echoed in my mind, drowning out the cheers from the previous weeks.

At seventeen, I felt as if I had lost everything. Football had been my identity, my refuge, and without it, I didn't know who I was anymore. It was as if the weight of my family's expectations and my own dreams had come crashing down on me all at once. I remember sitting in my room, staring blankly at the walls, consumed by despair. I had no hope. I would often say that I wasn't suicidal, but I wished I were dead because I felt I had nothing to live for.

Then, a card arrived from Pastor Darrell Scott. I'll never forget it. In his kind, handwritten note, he reminded me that God had a mighty purpose and plan for me, something greater than football. "Your future is as bright as the promises of God," he wrote. That message became my lifeline, an anchor for my soul. It was a turning point and a flicker of light in my darkest hour.

Shortly after, my life took a dramatic turn when I was involved in a terrible car accident. I rolled my truck during a snowstorm, breaking several vertebrae. The truck was crushed, and the gas tank had ruptured, spewing fuel everywhere. I should have died, but somehow, I survived. The police officer on the scene said I was one lucky kid. The doctors were baffled and called it a miracle. But lying there in the hospital, I didn't feel lucky. I felt broken and alone.

The doctors told me I might not walk again, let alone run or work out or play football. I remember the weight of their words hanging in the air, and I felt like I was spiraling down a dark tunnel. But then, I felt a sensation in my toes. It was faint but real, and with that small flicker of hope, I knew I had a choice. I could either succumb to despair or fight back with everything I had. I chose to fight. I remember thinking, "I'm going to walk. I'm going to run. I'm going to prove them wrong." The Bible says, "What is impossible with man is possible with God" (Luke 18:27), and that became my mantra every day in rehab.

Ten months after the accident, I was back to working out. I was at the gym, bench-pressing with my buddy. After my set, he warned me, "Hey, don't look over there. The preacher man is gonna try to save you."

So, of course, I looked. And there he was—a bald guy with a ring of hair, wearing a white V-neck T-shirt tucked into biker shorts and sporting a big gold watch. But he was jacked—completely fit. I turned to my buddy and asked, "Who is that guy?"

He replied, "That's Pastor Darrell Scott."

Before he could finish, I bolted across the gym. "Pastor Darrell!" I shouted, extending my hand. "I'm Paul. Awhile back, you sent me this beautiful card, telling me that my future was as bright as the promises of God. Thank you, thank you, thank you."

Pastor Darrell looked up to heaven and said, "Praise the Lord. Paul, every day I pray for divine appointments, and today's your day." Right there, in the middle of the gym, he began sharing the gospel with me. But I wasn't ready to hear it. I excused myself and went back to living life my way.

Three months later, I found myself at a crossroads. I was working full-time and attending school full-time, and after an evening class, I headed home, exhausted. The house I lived in with four roommates was often filled with chaos, and that night was no different. Cars lined the street. As I pulled into the driveway, I could hear music blaring, people laughing, and the clink of beer bottles. Inside, my roommates were partying like it was New Year's Eve. Something inside me snapped. I stormed in and threw everyone out, their shouts of "You're no fun anymore!" echoing as I stood in the wreckage of the night.

Alone, I stared at the mess, thinking, *There's got to be more to life than this.*

Then came a knock at the door.

Angry and seething, I marched to the door, ready to punch whoever was on the other side. When I flung it open, there stood Pastor Darrell, his breath visible in the cold air and a Bible clutched in his hand. "I was in the neighborhood," he said with a smile.

I was embarrassed. The house reeked of booze and bad choices. But Pastor Darrell didn't care. He stepped inside with a calm grace, looking past the chaos to see me. We sat down, and without hesitation, he began to talk to me about life, purpose, and faith. He told me that everyone has a God-shaped void in their heart, something we all try to fill with money, success, relationships—anything that promises fulfillment but never delivers. Only a relationship with Jesus Christ can fill that void.

That night, something changed. It wasn't just coincidence that brought Pastor Darrell there. It was a divine appointment. He saw me not as a broken man lost in the mess of life but as someone who still had hope, still had a chance. And sitting there in that wreck of a house, I started to believe it too. As he spoke, something broke inside me. I realized I had been trying to fill my life with things that couldn't satisfy—parties, success, anger. But that night, I finally understood: God was offering me a better way—HIS way.

"Paul," Pastor Darrell said softly, "God is knocking on the door of your heart, just like I knocked on your door tonight."

He led me in a simple prayer, asking God to come into my life, to forgive me for my sins, and to give me a new purpose. As I prayed, I felt a weight lifting, a door opening. The old was gone, and something new had begun (2 Cor. 5:17).

That night, in the middle of my messy, broken life, I made the most important decision I would ever make. God had knocked on the door of my heart, and I had finally let him in.

I knew then that my life had a purpose beyond what I could see. I felt God had spared my life for a reason, and that realization ignited a fire within me. Instead of wasting my time on things that didn't matter, I began to invest in others, particularly in my siblings, who were going through the same awful circumstances I had endured. I wanted to show them that life could be different.

Looking back, I see how God's hand guided me every step of the way. It wasn't always the path I planned, but it was the path I needed. I learned that even in the darkest moments, God is working out his purpose. When others "intended to harm me, . . . God intended it for good" (Gen. 50:20).

My life has been a testimony of grace, resilience, and hope. I now see the struggles I faced not as burdens but as stepping stones that forged me into the person I am today and led me to a future filled with promise. "In their hearts humans plan their course, but the Lord establishes their steps" (Prov. 16:9). And through it all, I have learned to trust in God's guidance, knowing that he is always leading me on a path of purpose: "For I know the plans I have for you, . . . plans to give you hope and a future" (Jer. 29:11).

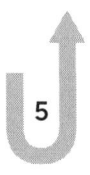

DEBRA BLEVONS

GUIDED BY GRACE

I grew up in a loving, church-centered family where faith was at the core of everything we did. Every time the doors of the church were open, we were there. My parents were devout, and their faith formed the foundation of our home life. But it wasn't until I was older that I truly experienced Jesus in a personal, life-changing way.

I'm the oldest of four, and when my younger brother was born, my mother suffered from what we now know as severe postpartum depression. Back then, it was treated as a nervous breakdown. She was hospitalized for months, undergoing shock treatments and other intense therapies. It was a difficult time for my family. So at eleven or twelve years old, I had to step up. I became responsible for my younger siblings and quickly learned to manage a household while still just a child myself.

This experience changed me. I became introverted and shy, more focused on my family's well-being than on school or socializing. I didn't get the best grades and often skipped out on social events because I needed to get home to take care of my siblings. Despite all of this, I knew I was growing stronger in ways I didn't fully understand at the time. And through it all, my faith deepened. It was my faith that helped me through every trial and challenge.

As I grew older, I didn't initially see myself as a career woman. I always thought I'd marry young and have children. But God had other plans for me. I didn't meet my husband, Greg, until I was forty, and we married when I was forty-five. Though I didn't have children of my own, I began to realize that God had given me a family in another way. My team at Northwestern Mutual became my extended family, and their growth and success became my greatest joys. I felt as if I was making an impact, not just in business but also in people's lives, helping them achieve dreams they never thought were possible.

My career began unexpectedly. I joined Northwestern Mutual in 1988 after leaving a stable middle-management job in banking. I had no idea that decision would lead me to a long, rewarding career in leadership. I wasn't a fast starter, and I certainly didn't have all the qualifications or credentials many of my colleagues did, but I knew I had a passion for helping others grow. That passion fueled me.

I eventually became the second female managing partner in Northwestern Mutual's history. It wasn't easy, and I faced many challenges as the only woman in that role for years. But I believed in leading with authenticity, with compassion and love for my people. My leadership wasn't just about reaching numbers or hitting goals. It was also about empowering others and being a servant leader, something I learned from Jesus's example.

One of the most profound trials in my life was when my husband and I were in a motorcycle accident during a managing partner conference in Arizona. We hit some debris on a blind corner, and the bike went down. I flew off the bike and slid across the road. Greg pulled me out of the path of an oncoming semitruck, and in that moment, I knew God had spared my life for a reason. Everything that followed—the ambulance that happened to be nearby, the quick medical care—was nothing short of a miracle.

Coming back from that accident wasn't easy. I suffered from PTSD, depression, and physical injuries that required months of therapy. My agency was struggling, and I wasn't in the mental or physical shape to lead effectively. My staff, in their love and care, encouraged me to seek help, which I did. I reached a point where I had to surrender everything to God. I remember lying face down in prayer, telling the Lord that if it was his will for me to leave Northwestern Mutual, I would do it. I was ready to give it all up—the position, the title, the income—because I knew God was enough.

But again, God had other plans. He wasn't done with me yet. Through that difficult season, my faith grew deeper, and five years later, my agency doubled in size. It was a testament to God's faithfulness and the power of surrender.

As I reflect on my life, I see how every trial, every hardship, and every unexpected turn was part of God's plan for me. I learned to lead by serving others, loving my team, and trusting in God's direction, even when it didn't make sense to me. My career may have felt accidental at times, but I know now that it was guided by God's hand all along.

After the accident, my journey as a leader completely shifted. I had always been something of a perfectionist, trying to control every detail in my work and life. But after going through such a humbling experience—physically, mentally, and spiritually—I began to see things differently. I learned the true value of servant leadership.

Before, I had thought leadership was about driving results, ensuring everything was done the right way—my way. But God used that season of my life to teach me that leadership is about serving others, empowering them to use their own gifts, and letting go of the need to control everything myself. My team carried me through when I wasn't at my best, and they showed me what it meant to work together with love and trust.

It was then that I fully embraced the idea that, as a leader, my role was to lift others up, to be the support they needed to reach their potential. I no longer saw myself as the one at the top of the pyramid giving orders. Instead, I wanted to be at the base, holding my team up, helping them succeed. Jesus's example of washing his disciples' feet became my model. Leadership was about humility, about being there for my people—not just professionally but personally as well.

In every leadership meeting, I made it a point to ask my managing directors, "How are you loving your people today?" It wasn't a question they were used to hearing in a corporate setting, but to me, love was the core of everything. I wanted them to lead with compassion, with the same care and grace that I had experienced from my own team when I was at my lowest. I wanted our company culture to reflect something deeper than just numbers and success. I wanted it to be about making a difference in the lives of others.

One of the most rewarding parts of my career was seeing my team thrive. I remember when one of my advisers, a woman in the Upper Peninsula of Michigan, showed me the fruits of her hard work. She invited me to her home on a beautiful lake. She pointed to her house and said, "This is my dream come true—a home for my family—something I never thought I'd have." She told me that Northwestern Mutual and the belief I had in her made it possible. That moment reminded me of why I had chosen this path, why I kept pushing forward even when things were hard.

As time went on, I felt God calling me into a new season of life. After twenty-one years as a managing partner, I knew it was time to step down and make way for new leadership.

Now, as Greg and I spend more time together, I'm reminded of how important it is to balance work with life.

For so many years, I poured myself into my career, often at the expense of other things. But now I see the value of slowing down, of enjoying the simple moments—whether it's a quiet morning by the lake, a long walk with our dogs, or time spent with family and friends. Life is precious and is fuller now in ways I never imagined. I'm learning to savor every moment, knowing that each one is a gift from God.

My journey has been filled with unexpected turns, challenges I never saw coming, and blessings I couldn't have anticipated. When I look back, I see how God was shaping me, how each trial, each triumph, and every unexpected detour had a purpose. Through it all, God has been faithful. He's led me every step of the way, and for that, I am eternally grateful. My story isn't one of career success but one of faith—faith that God knows what he's doing even when we don't. Faith that, in the end, all things work together for good.

I have learned that our plans, no matter how carefully laid, are often redirected by God's hand. My life is a testament to that. I never planned to be in leadership, to move to Atlanta, or to take on the responsibilities that came my way. I certainly didn't plan to face a near-fatal accident or wrestle with PTSD. But each of these moments has become a part of my story, woven into the fabric of who I am. And every time, God met me in those places with grace, showing me that his plan was far better than anything I could have imagined.

Though I'm no longer in the office every day, I still feel connected to the work God has called me to do—

empowering others and sharing the love of Christ in everything I do. One of the greatest joys in this season has been giving back. Whether through our nonprofit work or in mentoring others and helping them to rise and thrive, I've found that there's nothing more fulfilling than using the gifts and resources God has given us to bless others.

One of the things I always tell my mentees is to trust in God's timing. It's easy to get frustrated when things don't happen as quickly as we'd like or when doors seem to close. But I've learned that every closed door, every delay, is part of a larger plan. I think back to the moments when I doubted myself or felt like giving up, and I see now that God was using those moments to build my character, teach me perseverance, and prepare me for what was ahead.

Greg and I have been particularly passionate about helping children, and we've been involved in a ministry that decorates rooms for children battling cancer. It's a small way to bring a little joy and light into a difficult time, and it's been a blessing to be a part of that work.

As I look to the future, I know there will be more challenges and unexpected turns, but I'm at peace with whatever comes. God has brought me this far, and I trust that he will continue to guide me. My life has been a journey of faith guided by his grace, and I'm excited to see where he leads me next.

In the end, my story isn't about the titles I've held or the achievements I've earned. It's about the faith that has carried me through, the people I've had the privilege to walk alongside, and the grace that has shaped my life. I'm grateful for every moment—every joy, every trial, and every lesson. It's all part of the story God is writing, and I wouldn't have it any other way.

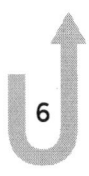

JOHN QUALY

MOVING GOD FROM THE TRUNK TO THE DRIVER'S SEAT

I wasn't always a man of faith. In fact, for most of my life, I believed in God the way some people believe in the idea of gravity: I knew he existed, but I didn't give him much thought beyond that. My view of God was skewed. I saw him as demanding and conditional, just waiting for me to mess up so he could exact his judgment. And who would want to get close to someone like that?

So I did what I think a lot of people do. I put God in the trunk of my car, neatly tucked away like a spare tire, something I would reach for only when things went terribly wrong. And for the most part, that seemed to work. Life was going well. I signed my first contract with Northwestern Mutual as a college agent in 1969, right around the time humans were landing on the moon and the United States was involved in the Vietnam War. While the world was shooting for the stars and at each other, I was focused on my own life goals: growing a successful business and building what I thought would bring me true joy and satisfaction.

In 1973, I started a scratch district agency in Columbia, Missouri. I grew it from a single college intern to five Million Dollar Round Table qualifiers. In 1990, I was appointed managing partner in St. Louis. The agency had 46 representatives and was producing $5 million in premium. By the end of 2010, the agency had grown to 198 representatives, and we were pulling in over $30 million in premium. We did 14,820 lives, and no agency has done that since. On paper, my life seemed to be going really well. But inside me, something was missing. The hole inside me—the one I tried to fill with success, recognition, and wealth—was only getting bigger. I felt hollow.

I was still driving the car of my life, but the road was getting bumpier. Every time I hit a bump in the road, I'd reach back to the trunk where I kept God and ask him to come sit in the backseat. I'd tell him, "Alright, I'm facing a rough patch here; I could use some help." And after the crisis passed, I'd politely tell him to get back in the trunk, and I'd continue on my way. I didn't realize then how backward my approach to faith really was.

As the years passed, my life became more and more about achieving business milestones, hitting numbers, and outperforming the competition. But there were cracks forming under the surface—cracks I couldn't ignore. Fear, anxiety, and uncertainty began creeping in. On the outside, I tried to keep it all together, but inside, I was struggling to hold the pieces of my life in place.

In 2000, two events shook me to my core and changed everything.

The first involved my daughter Madison. One winter evening, my wife, Kathy, and I took Madison to the park to sled after a fresh snowfall. As she raced down the hill on a saucer sled, she lost control and slammed into a tree. Panicked, I started running to her side. As I tended to Madison, a young boy came over and asked me a question that would echo in my mind for months: "Hey mister, what church do you go to?"

What church did I go to? Though my wife had been going to church regularly, I was always too busy. I hadn't thought about it in years. The question lingered long after Madison was safe, and it nudged something deep inside me. The following Sunday, for the first time in what felt like forever, I went to church. I didn't know it at the time, but the small act of stepping into that building was the beginning of a much larger journey.

Just months later, my brother Bill passed away. His death was like a sledgehammer to my already shaky sense of control. I was the oldest, the first in line in our family, and now my younger brother was gone. As I sat with my father in the living room of our home the morning of the funeral, Pastor George, who had come to pray with us, asked a simple yet profound question: "Do you know how to get into heaven?" My father and I exchanged looks and gave the only answer we knew: "You live a good life, be a good person, take care of others."

The pastor smiled gently and said, "It's by the grace and blood of Jesus Christ."

I can't explain it, but in that moment, it was as if a veil had been lifted. For years, I had been trying to live "a good life," to achieve success and be "a good person." But here, in the face of my brother's death, I realized how little control I really had. Getting to heaven isn't about my achievements or my version of goodness. It is about something much bigger—something I couldn't accomplish on my own.

I started meeting with Pastor George regularly. Slowly, over time, I began to understand what faith really is. It isn't about keeping God in the trunk for emergencies. It's about giving him the wheel, letting him drive the car of my life, and trusting him completely—even when the road ahead looks uncertain. It's communicating with God daily and being thankful in both good times and difficult times.

I'm a late bloomer when it comes to faith, but I'm deeply grateful that I know Jesus as my Lord and Savior. I am catching up fast, and my life now is filled with a purpose and a peace I never knew existed. I still experience fear and anxiety at times, but I've learned that I don't have to face them alone. God's no longer in the trunk—he's now in the driver's seat, steering me through every twist and turn.

Looking back, I see now how blind and unaware I was. I spent years chasing idols—success, recognition, wealth—believing they would bring me fulfillment, but all they gave me was fleeting happiness. I know now that true joy and true peace come from something far greater than anything I could ever achieve on my own.

I've been attending the Christian Fellowship Breakfasts since the late '80s, driven by a sense that I needed to be there. However, my true involvement began in 2006 when I received a call from Jim Milonas, and that moment forever impacted my life. The Christian Fellowship Community is a community of faith, deep connection, learning, and transformational growth. It has been one of the most meaningful things I have been a part of, and I am deeply thankful.

And that's my story. It's not perfect, and my story's not done yet! But every day, I wake up and choose to let God lead. I'm no longer driving into the ditch because I finally put him where he belongs: at the center of it all.

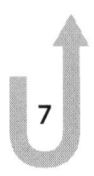

RON JOELSON

YOUR TURNING POINT OPPORTUNITY

The powerful testimonies and faith journeys of the six people who have shared their stories in this book are nothing less than inspiring. They are stories of hardships and blessings, fear and faith, serving people versus serving God, eternal doubt and eternal assurance, and God's perfect love and perfect justice. Throughout all these stories, the victories of Jesus Christ have come shining through. These individuals were overcome by the world at various times but are now themselves overcomers through Christ! While Jesus Christ is the real hero, each of them continues his work as they share their stories. Christ works differently in each of our lives, and yet there are patterns that reflect the never-changing nature of God. These stories are a testament to God's faithfulness to and patience with each of his children. How wonderful that our Christian Fellowship Community (CFC) was inspired to compile these six testimonies from our CFC Forum Zoom calls into a book we can hold in our hands and in our hearts!

If you had told me prior to my involvement with CFC that there was a book about these six individuals, I might have assumed it was about how to succeed as a financial adviser at Northwestern Mutual. Each of them has had a successful professional career that anyone would be proud of. Certainly, there is a link between our spiritual and professional lives. We are meant to live abundant lives (John 10:10). But their success as defined by the world's standards is not the focus of these stories, nor is their identity defined by their financial success. Each one understands that they are first and foremost a child of the Most High God and a citizen of heaven who will occupy this earth for only a short time. In the meantime, we continue to work until Jesus returns (Luke 19:13).

No doubt, young and inexperienced advisers would benefit professionally from spending time with these people. But the lessons learned in this book are far more valuable and for a much greater purpose. They point to the meaning, reward, and fulfillment of a life in Christ, both in this world and in the one to come. And together, they present the gospel in a compelling way.

There are biblical principles in Scripture for achieving financial success in this life, though there are not many. But the focus in this book is on the heart, and having one's heart right with God is a critical first step to success, financial or otherwise.

For example, in "The Journey of Truth," Philip Sarnecki had a heart change when he understood that salvation is a gift that cannot be earned and is not deserved by human beings. He quotes Ephesians 2:8–9: "For it is by grace you have been saved, through faith—and this is not from yourselves, it is the gift of God—not by works, so that no one can boast." Philip recognized that Christ's death on the cross covered everything and that his own works, in comparison, could never be sufficient. Besides, if he could earn salvation, then it would no longer be a gift! He also quotes Romans 3:23: "All have sinned and fall short of the glory of God." Though Philip was a rule follower and self-proclaimed "good kid," he realized he could never be good enough and could never save himself. Thus, the need for a Savior.

Gerard Hempstead echoed that sentiment in "My Journey of Transformation," though his background was very different. He experienced real hypocrisy when trying to hold to his parents' strong Christian values while slipping into sin at college. He was ashamed of the double life he was living, and he believed the enemy's lies that he was unworthy of God's love. He later came to realize that though he was still a sinner, Christ yet loved him—enough to die for him (Rom. 5:8). This realization that God's love was unconditional was a game changer!

While grace abounds in Philip's and Gerard's stories, there is a lot about God's justice in John Folkert's testimony, "Overcoming Fear." In fact, John was terrified.

He recognized that God's perfect justice would condemn him because he knew he could never live up to God's standards. Attending church, learning catechism, and doing other good deeds could not offset his misdeeds, which would disqualify him. Those transgressions would render a guilty verdict from a "terrifying" God whose standard is perfection: "Be perfect, therefore, as your heavenly Father is perfect" (Matt. 5:48). Even one lie would render a guilty verdict. Fortunately, John learned that Jesus Christ was the bridge between God's perfect love and his perfect justice. Although God was to be feared with awe and reverence, he was not terrifying after all! In fact, "he was pierced for our transgressions, he was crushed for our iniquities; . . . and by his wounds we are healed" (Isa. 53:5).

When John learned that Jesus was born to die and that Jesus paid the penalty for his sins, he was able to finally rest in Christ! It was as if someone walked into the courtroom of heaven and paid all the fines necessary to cover John's sins. Only a good God who loves his children would do such a thing. Today, John's good works are done not to earn a heavenly reward but out of gratitude for what John was given! His goals are no longer worldly goals but spiritual ones. Now he longs to one day hear, "Well done, good and faithful servant!" (Matt. 25:21). He knows that his salvation is not about anything he has done but about everything Christ has done.

The theme of God's love is impactful in Paul Ludacka's testimony, "A Path Guided by God." He faced real childhood trauma, including verbal abuse and violence.

In anger, his stepfather called him "worthless" and much worse. Not surprisingly, Paul sought love and acceptance through performance, such as success in school, sports, and the things of this world. That conditional love fell apart after one sports mishap. Only the unconditional love of Jesus Christ could permanently fill the hole in his heart. We may not have experienced the dramatic circumstances of Paul's childhood, but each of us has the same need for unconditional love. We are made for a love relationship with an all-powerful God!

How did these individuals receive all that Jesus Christ was ready to give them? By faith. Or as it says more specifically in Ephesians 2:8, they received it "by grace . . . through faith." When Philip Sarnecki understood that faith was his new foundation, his life changed. The difference wasn't just that Philip had faith that Jesus was real. Rather, Philip had faith that he could trust Jesus for his salvation. His good works were a result of his salvation and not the way to receive it.

As Debra Blevons explains in her story, "Guided by Grace," God's faithfulness is continuous. Salvation is not only about eternal security but also about God's faithfulness, which had brought her through every aspect of her life. Every trial was a lesson, and every frustration was replaced with an understanding that it was part of God's plan. It wasn't that God caused the problems but rather that "in all things God works for the good of those who love him, who have been called according to his purpose" (Rom. 8:28). Her leadership and service became her way of sharing with others how God was impacting her life. Gerard also sees service as his calling and the guiding principle of his life. Only Jesus Christ could have transformed these people!

Unquestionably, the life stories shared in this book have pointed toward Jesus Christ. He is the most important person in each story. But I see something else emerging from these testimonies and from knowing these people personally. They do not separate their spiritual lives from their professional lives. They do not limit God to one hour on Sundays and spend the rest of their time on other things. God has been interwoven right into the fabric of their lives. They don't ask if they are devoting enough time to God because they put God in the middle of every aspect of their lives. John Qualy's testimony, "Moving God from the Trunk to the Driver's Seat," is an excellent example of how someone realizes that Jesus is not only their Savior but also Lord of their life! John understands that if Jesus was hitchhiking and he picked him up, he wouldn't put him in the trunk. Jesus would drive! And so today, Jesus drives his life, and John diligently follows as best he can.

Imagine what our lives would look like if we brought God into our work, our families, and our relationships? What if God were a part of our businesses, our government, our sources of entertainment, and our educational institutions? Perhaps the church has even encouraged the isolationism we see from Christians who do not want to offend others. But the gospel offends (Mark 8:31–33 and elsewhere), and the people in this book are willing to risk offending others to show the love of Christ. Christians want the people of the world to understand that when we share the good news of the kingdom of God, we are not condemning them but speaking out of love for them. We want others to know God personally because we love them.

Perhaps you, the reader, have been inspired by these stories. As it was for each of these individuals, you too can at any time receive Jesus Christ into your heart and declare him Lord of your life. The Bible says, "If you declare with your mouth, 'Jesus is Lord,' and believe in your heart that God raised him from the dead, you will be saved" (Rom. 10:9). But doing so requires that you acknowledge your need of a savior. God's standard of perfection means that if we have lied or cheated or stolen or failed to help others (I could go on), we are sinners. Jesus took it further and said that when we are angry with someone, it is tantamount to committing murder, and that a lustful thought is no different from having actually committed adultery (Matt. 5:21–22, 27–28).

The penalty for sin is death: "The wages of sin is death," but Jesus's death on the cross provided payment for our sin: "The gift of God is eternal life in Christ Jesus" (Rom. 6:23). Jesus Christ is the ultimate expression of God's love. Jesus, who knew no sin, literally became sin for us on the cross. He was and is both God and man at the same time! Someone once said, "He was so much a man it was as though he was not God at all, and so much God it was as though he was not man at all. He was God's perfect man and man's perfect God!"

If salvation is a gift, all that is left for us to do is to receive it, to accept his payment for our transgressions, past, present, and future—and we do this by faith. Faith is not merely believing that God and Jesus are real. Even the devil believes that! Rather, faith is putting our trust completely in God and in what Jesus did on the cross for our eternal security. If you believe this sincerely, then you can pray as follows:

> *Father God, I know that I am a sinner and that I cannot save myself. I know that you are a loving God who wants an eternal relationship with me. But you are also a just God who requires payment for all my sins against you. So I thank you for sending your son, Jesus Christ, who died on the cross and then rose from the dead to pay the penalty for my sin and purchase a place for me in heaven, all of which you have provided as a gift. I receive this gift through faith by trusting in Jesus Christ alone for my salvation. Jesus, I receive you now as my Savior and the Lord of my life.*

If you have prayed this earnestly and sincerely, I welcome you into the family of God! You have the same heavenly position as each of the six people who shared their stories in this book and as countless others! Now, the motive for godly living is gratitude for all that Christ has accomplished on your behalf.

The last part of the prayer is critical. Acknowledging that Jesus is Lord of your life is significant. It is a game changer! Through the Holy Spirit, you will be convicted of sin, and your behavior will change over time because of your desire to please your Father (even though your eternal security has been settled). In fact, you will find that you are motivated to repent, literally, "turn from" your sin as the Spirit reveals it to you because of Jesus's willingness to die for you. Ending the sinful behavior becomes as important to you as it is to him.

Like those who shared their testimonies, you too will experience a radical heart change! Over time, your heart will begin to look a lot like God's, and when he gives you the desires of your heart (Ps. 37:4), you will find that your desires match his desires for you!

A great first step in your walk of faith is to dive into your Bible and reach out to connect with me or any of those whose story is shared in this book. Many new Christians start with the book of John because it not only describes what happened to Jesus but also emphasizes who he is. You have read the testimonies of six individuals who know Jesus Christ. Now, read the Bible and get to know God for yourself. It's time to find out what your Creator has to say! How can you follow Jesus if you don't know much about him or what he has said? It's never too late to find out!

Connect with the CFC

Christian Fellowship Breakfasts

Attend the Christian Fellowship Breakfasts, held every January, February, and July, to foster community within Network Offices and be inspired by a speaker's story.

CFC Study Groups

Join a CFC Study Group, meeting weekly across the country, to grow together in Christian community and deepen your journey as a disciple of Jesus.

Register for these opportunities & more at:
www.christianfellowshipcommunity.org

CFC Forum

Participate in the monthly CFC Forum, hosted by Ron Joelson, where a guest speaker shares their pivotal turning point in their life journey.

Prayer Gathering

Partake in relational, spontaneous, and Spirit-led prayer on the biweekly CFC Prayer Gathering with John Qualy and Wade Burleson.

Questions? Email:
brittany@christianfellowshipcommunity.org

THE HISTORY
OF THE
CHRISTIAN FELLOWSHIP COMMUNITY

The Christian Fellowship Community (CFC) began in 1967 when Roy Beamer, a Northwestern Mutual Insurance representative, brought together a dozen like-minded individuals for breakfast ahead of the company's annual meeting. What started as a simple gathering quickly became an annual event. Each summer, talented, energetic, and imaginative leaders contributed to planning and leading these events, forming a vibrant community that profoundly impacted lives.

In the early 1980s, the Christian Fellowship Community Breakfast was moved to large hotels in downtown Milwaukee to accommodate its growing attendance. Additional innovations such as transitioning to the Baird Center, introducing table hosts, and involving key representatives and managing partners fueled this growth even further.

By the year 2000, CFC had expanded beyond Milwaukee's annual meeting to organized regional gatherings across the nation. These events featured prominent speakers who brought energy, celebrity appeal, and a faithful Christian witness, drawing larger audiences and deepening the impact of the community.

Heather Whitestone, Miss America 1995
Dan Reeves, NFL Head Coach
Dr. Ben Carson
Ken Blanchard, Author "One Minute Manager"
Jon Gordon, Author of "The Energy Bus"
Thomas Rhett & Lauren Akins

2024 Milwaukee Christian Fellowship Community Luncheon

Today, the Christian Fellowship Community extends far beyond its events, forming authentic communities. The Christian Fellowship Community Forum now has over 2,300 registered participants who engage in monthly virtual gatherings. Hosted by Ron Joelson, these forums feature special guests from the Northwestern Mutual family, fostering fellowship and inspiration.

Each June, Keith Wagner, Northwestern Mutual's leading producer from 2011–2024, hosts a complimentary webinar tailored to interns and representatives with under five years of experience. This year, over 4,000 individuals from Network Offices attended the event.

Additionally, thanks to the generosity of the managing partners, the Keith Wagner Lecture Series features a special guest annually and attracts 5,000–6,000 attendees each year.

Local Christian Fellowship Community Study Groups have also flourished, meeting regularly in Network Offices and the Home Office to grow in faith and community. New groups are launching every week, further expanding their impact.

CFC's leadership, including its board of directors, gathers annually at Jeff Reeter's ranch in Texas for renewal and reflection. This time together allows them to envision new ways the Christian Fellowship Community can continue to grow and serve its members and can have an even greater impact.

The Christian Fellowship Community is more than just breakfast events. It is a movement dedicated to fostering meaningful relationships, supporting personal and spiritual growth, and creating opportunities to live out the Christian faith in every sphere of life.

As we look ahead, we see a future filled with new and exciting opportunities. Thank you for being a part of this journey with us!

2025 CFC
BOARD OF DIRECTORS

Dwaan Black
Wade Burleson
Steven Dugal
Bob Erkel
Gerard Hempstead
Ron Joelson
Mark Kull
Kevin Lawhon
Jim Milonas
John Qualy
Jeff Reeter
Keith Wagner
Conrad York

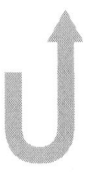

All of the stories in this book originated from the Christian Fellowship Community Forum monthly sessions.

Hear more stories like this from Tim Gerend, Jon Gordon, Kim Schlifske, and others here at this link:

christianfellowshipcommunity.org/cfc-forum

Thank you to all who have participated in this
CFC publishing endeavor.

**Christian
Fellowship
Community**